Ms Gayle Bondy
1432 Floyd
Modesto, CA 95355

First Printing — August, 1981
Second Printing — January, 1982

Copyright © 1981 by Dr. Terry Chitwood

ISBN 0-942044-00-2

Published by:
POLESTAR PUBLICATIONS
620 South Minnesota Avenue
Sioux Falls, SD 57104

How To Defend Yourself Without Even Trying

By
Dr. Terry Chitwood

POLESTAR Publications • Sioux Falls, South Dakota

ACKNOWLEDGMENTS

The person responsible for helping me come up with the idea for this book was a spiritual master who retired, better known as my wife, Deb. I want to thank you for finding the mistakes that I did not want to find and making me correct them. Without your spiritual guidance the book would not have been written.

I want to thank my aikido students for pretending to fall when I throw them and my self-mastery students for keeping their sessions interesting. And, as Steve Martin says, "I want to thank each and every one of you. Thank you, thank you, thank you, thank you, thank you . . ."

CONTENTS

Dedication
Quote
Prologue

MIND

Attitude   49
Nonattachment   51
Quality   53

THE BEGINNING

My Early Years   13
My Later Years   16
My Future Years   19

SPIRIT

Intuition   59
Power   61
Presence   63

PERCEPTION

Space   23
Time   25
Telepathy 27

MARTIAL ARTS

Study   69
Belts   70
Ki   72

BODY

Energy   33
Emptiness   34
Relaxing   35

GAMES

Being Centered   77
Robots   79
Go   81

EMOTION

Fear   41
Devotion   43
Humor   45

THE WAY

Nonviolence   85
Friendship   87
Self-Mastery   89

This book is dedicated to:

Master Uyeshiba
Master Tohei
and George Breed
who taught me
the essence of
aikido without
even trying.

"There is no form and no style
in Aikido. The movement of Aikido
is the movement of Nature — whose secret
is profound and infinite."

— Master Uyeshiba*

*Uyeshiba, Kisshomaru, *Aikido,* Tokyo, Hozansha
Publishing Co., Ltd., p. 169.

PROLOGUE

Although I have been practicing aikido for most of my life, I was first consciously introduced to it in 1974 by Dr. George Breed, who studied with Master Tohei. After practicing and developing its principles for three years, I had an exciting and amazing discovery during the summer of 1977.

One night when I was asleep but not asleep, I found myself on another level of consciousness studying aikido with Master Uyeshiba, the founder of aikido. At the end of the lesson he told me that I must teach. I cried tears of gratitude and devotion as I accepted an initiation that was to provide a sense of power and direction to my life.

Since that day I have taught aikido and have always been guided by a power greater than myself. Even hitchhikers during the length of their rides study aikido with me. The universe rules my life and has brought me a gift that I would like to share with you: the harmony of nonviolence or more humorously put, "How to Defend Yourself Without Even Trying."

*"...the universe
is miraculous in its power
to transform the individual."*

The Beginning

MY EARLY YEARS

I wish I could say I came out of the womb riding on a stream of energy. However, it simply was not so dramatic. My birth was more of a not-doing, where I learned how to be calm under stress.

My mother was a nervous woman and, not being completely at one with having me, she had a prolonged labor. So my first aikido lesson was learning to be relaxed while being stuck in the womb with the walls contracting and squeezing my newly formed body. That day taught me an important lesson: Relax and let go and you will survive.

My early years were uneventful from the standpoint of lots of physical action taking place, but teaching took place on a subtle level. My grandfather is a gentle and wise man who taught me silence and appreciation of the beauty of nature. Watching and feeding the ducks at the lake was one of my first meditations.

Being introduced to the educational system or, "how to make yourself into a brainless robot in twelve years without even trying," was a suffocating experience. Not only were the teachers not aware of a greater reality, but the students thought that physical force ruled the world. I remember effortlessly brushing aside their attacks with movements that came to me spontaneously. Somehow they always ended up on the ground, but neither of us got hurt.

Once a local gang tried to terrorize me by threatening me with knives. I intuitively knew that I would not be hurt, so I was unafraid. Their fun was over before it started. Such people feed on fear. After that encounter I began a slow jog home. I had covered some distance when their leader decided it might be fun to chase me (perhaps he perceived my running as fear). As he approached, I stopped jogging and felt a great sense of peace overtake me. It was as if the sky opened and a voice telepathically assured me that I would be alright. So I stood my ground. As the gang gathered around me their leader approached me, grabbed my right arm with both hands, and with all his might tried to throw me into a ditch. When my body remained immovable, a surprised and frightened look appeared on his face. He rapidly felt my biceps with both hands and became more surprised. I was just a skinny kid. I guess he had no choice but to start making friendly jokes to let me know that I was okay. That was his first aikido lesson.

While in high school, I met similar situations with similar results. One incident stands out. Being a quiet and bright adolescent made me a perfect target for another gang. At the swimming pool about eight of them attempted to drown me. They did not know that water is the perfect element for practicing aikido. Needless to say, our workout together left them breathless and perplexed.

I never did consciously understand how I pulled off those fascinating incidents. Only years later when I was introduced to aikido did I make the connection.

MY LATER YEARS

Although I studied and taught judo and karate from 1965 to 1974, those experiences were not as meaningful as my aikido training and especially my teaching.

My aikido training from 1974–1977 can be summarized by saying that I rediscovered what I already knew. After my experience with Master Uyeshiba on a different plane of consciousness in 1977, I taught aikido to students in Iowa, Arizona, and South Dakota.

In Arizona I taught aikido to hard-core convicts in my prison rehabilitation program at the Fort Grant Training Center. This was a profound and enjoyable experience for me. These men were exceptionally receptive to new ways of being. Once they saw that inner energy is stronger than physical force, I had one-sixth of the prison population as my aikido students.

One man in particular stands out. He was a seven-time offender, an ex-Green Beret karate instructor, and a biker (with a bad temper). He had violent thoughts toward the assistant warden of security. He "hated him with a passion." When the inmate realized that his hate was only hurting himself, he no longer allowed the warden to control him by pressing his hate button. Thereafter, he would remain unaffected by the warden's provocative behavior.

The inmate became totally calm in tense situations with guards and others. He was in control of his own mind and it showed. When he was released from prison he went into a bar in Tucson where a man tried to pick a fight with him. Instead of annihilating the man, he made a friend of him. Another victory for the power of love and harmony.

After my work with convicts, I taught aikido in Phoenix. One memorable experience is a ki development class for children taught by one of my students, Jim. Jim conveyed the principles of harmony so well that a six-year-old boy was totally transformed. This boy was having emotional problems as well as problems with his school work. He had seen more than one psychologist. After his experience with a four-week ki class — just six hours of training — his school work improved and he was a happier and calmer child. Everyone noticed the dramatic change. His mother was so impressed that she had Jim continue to give her son private lessons.

Presently, I teach aikido in Sioux Falls, South Dakota and wherever else I happen to be. My students stand out as individuals who are engaged in the evolution of their consciousness and mastery of self. They are not concerned with belts, competition, and other forms of self-delusion. I am thankful to be able to teach such highly motivated and evolved individuals.

MY FUTURE YEARS

This book is part of my future and possibly your future. I wrote it for you in order to have you contemplate the way in which you are presently perceiving reality. I know that the universe is miraculous in its power to transform the individual. My life has been a series of miracles, and I hope to convey that yours can be filled with the same wonder.

In the years ahead, I plan to be part of the transformation of my present students and future students. Those of you on the path of self-knowledge who are inspired by this book may feel drawn to contact me. Please do so. You are my future students. Without you, my purpose would not be complete. You bring hope to this planet and play a most important part in fulfilling its destiny. Value yourselves highly for you will become living examples of a better way.

*"We are all
telepathically connected."*

Perception

SPACE

Think about how the area around your body affects your experience. If you lived in Vietnam during the late sixties, you would have been involved in a war and could possibly have been killed. On the other hand, a piece of personal space in rural South Dakota may have granted you a less dangerous and more harmonious life. Similarly, compare city life to country life. If you choose to move to or visit a city, you subject yourself to the experiences governing the city...probably more pollution, crime, and a more tense atmosphere. Living in the wrong city might subject you to death from a lung disease or as a victim of a violent crime. Whereas living in the country, you might live a long and peaceful life. You can see that where you place your body can mean the difference between life and death.

In aikido, it is important to pick your space if you have to defend yourself. If you feel drawn to stand in a certain place when defending, then do so. That place will give you more personal power to help you in your defense. When practicing aikido on the mats, students will be strong when standing

23

on certain parts and weak on others. Some parts of the mats are neutral zones. Unbelievable? Try it.

Power spots can be a few feet or many miles in diameter. Your power spots may not be the same as your friends'. If everyone's power spots were the same, people would be stacked up on top of each other living in only certain areas. The rest of the land would be empty. The universe is more orderly than that, so there is a more uniform distribution of people.

However, you may want to contemplate the commonality that attracts people to certain cities or areas within a city. Especially if you feel attracted to a certain space containing a large group of people, you may want to discover your connection with the people presently occupying that space. You may find it fascinating.

Power spots can affect your whole life. Ideally, you should live and work in places that give you power. Develop your awareness to discover your own power spots. They are different for everyone.

TIME

Time is not always constant. It can expand and contract. When time expands, you experience a slowing down of other people's movements and you can still move at your usual speed. When time contracts, everyone around you appears to be moving more rapidly and your movements are slow and uncoordinated.

I first noticed time expansion when I was matching multiple opponents during karate class. My opponents' movements were in slow motion, and I could easily step aside or block their punches or kicks. After the match I thought, "Now this is the state of mind to be pursued. What use are all of my fancy punches, kicks, and blocks when I can effortlessly avoid attacks by achieving that state of mind." My cultivation of that state eventually led to my study of aikido.

The ability to expand time has a lot to do with relaxed concentration. If you place your attention on a rapidly moving object and try hard to see the continuity of its movement, you will find that there will be gaps in your perception. You are dividing your attention between the moving object and your thoughts of trying hard. Your attention bounces from the object to your thought and back to the object, leaving a perceptual gap.

Instead, place your attention on the object but do not attempt to see it. The feeling that you experience when doing this is one of almost looking in the other direction. You need to "not care" if you perceive the object or not. Then not only will the perceptual gap be eliminated, but the object will appear to be moving in slow motion.

Do not be frustrated if you try this a few times and do not experience it immediately. It may take years of slowing down your thoughts through appropriate meditation and other practices before you can consciously control this state. However, if you completely understand the essence of what has been said and do not interfere with yourself, you can easily perform it the first time. And once you have performed it, you can repeat it by attaining the same state of mind that allowed you to initially perform it. Cultivate that state of mind.

TELEPATHY

We are all telepathically connected. Have you ever found yourself hearing the phone ring and knowing who is calling you before you pick up the receiver? Or have you needed to talk to someone and then met them that day in an unexpected place? If you contemplate your life, you may be able to find numerous examples of telepathy occurring.

There are no accidents. Dismissing telepathy as a chance occurrence is the tool the mind uses to maintain its tenuous hold on its personal structures of reality. Reality is multileveled and open-ended. Telepathic occurrences are commonplace within it.

Have you ever felt a bodily ailment or pain that you have never felt before? Possibly you are picking up someone else's symptoms. They resonate in your body until you identify who they belong to, and then they instantaneously disappear. Many people unconsciously channel other people's thoughts, feelings, and bodily reactions — especially those of people close to them such as parents and friends. If you have a job dealing with people, observe your bodily feelings when a person is in your presence. If you allow yourself an open mind, you may find yourself experiencing different bodily feelings around different people. You will be experiencing their feelings.

How does that apply to aikido? The ultimate self-defense is to telepathically sense the aggressive thoughts of another and to redirect them before the attack begins. Second best is sensing the person's inharmonious and aggressive vibrations and avoiding them.

After all, many attacks are initiated by the victim. If a person is feeling bad about himself and unconsciously desires to be hurt, he will draw his attacker to himself. Or instead, he may just have a car accident or some other injury. So it is important to know yourself thoroughly. Otherwise, you may find yourself telepathically contributing to your own attack.

*"...let streams of energy
flow off your fingertips..."*

Body

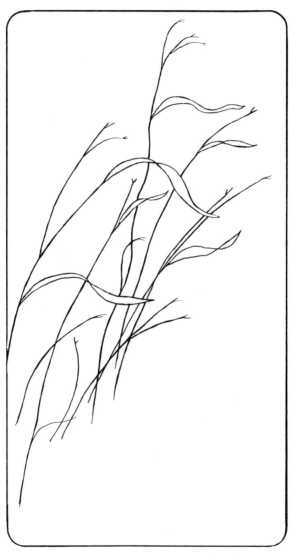

ENERGY

When you are walking down the street, let streams of energy flow off your fingertips caressing the path and people in front of you. Allow your body to become light like you are being lifted by a silken thread attached to the back of your head. Let your knees relax and feel the spring in your step.

What you are doing is practicing a basic principle of aikido, extending energy (ki). During any activity in which you engage, let the energy flow out the front of your body.

Sometime you may want to go for a walk and let the energy's pull guide you through town. As you drift like a cloud through the streets, you are guided by a power greater than yourself. You may end up meeting some interesting people and experiencing an excitement that you never thought possible. Follow the road sign that says, "Let the universe be your guide."

EMPTINESS

Let your thoughts settle and your mind become like a clear lake. Experience the feeling of emptiness. There is no internal dialogue between the various aspects of yourself, just complete calm. As you rest in emptiness, allow your intuition to send you important messages. Sense each message with your mind like a wave rolling up on a clear beach.

Experience a hollow bamboo flute in the center of your upper torso aligned from your head to your pelvic floor. Let all of the excess tension locked in your head and shoulders drain down the hollow tube to settle in your one point, located approximately one inch below your navel.

Feel your energy congregating in your one point as your body becomes powerful. You are now immovable and unliftable. Begin walking, you have stability and balance.

Practice placing your attention on the one point during your daily activities, then you will begin experiencing emptiness. Just like an empty cup remains ready to be filled, your life will be more fulfilled. Let the universe fill you instead of your internal chatter, then you will become tranquil and complete.

RELAXING

Observe your shoulders during your daily routine. Do you find them inching upward as the day progresses? This posture can contribute to a variety of headaches as well as pain in the neck region. You waste precious energy holding your shoulders in a contracted and rigid position.

Instead, consciously relax your shoulders and let them fall to a natural and relaxed posture. You may have to do this many times in the beginning. However, once you become aware of how and when you tense that region, you will be able to relax immediately.

Observe the other parts of your body, examining them for excessive tension. Be aware of your jaw. Let it drop so that your mouth is slightly open. Sense your abdomen. Are you unconsciously pulling it in? If so, let your abdomen relax so that your breath can fill it during the inhale.

Stand and let the muscles of your buttocks become relaxed. Be aware of how you are standing. Are your knees locked? Bend them slightly, even when you are walking.

Now visualize your breath flowing up through

the soles of your feet when you inhale. Let it continue through your body, caressing and relaxing each cell until it reaches your heart region. Then exhale through the top of your head. Let your exhale extend up through the sky, into space, and to the ends of the universe.

"...experience a profound thankfulness in your heart..."

Emotion

FEAR

Letting go of fear can dramatically change your life. Fear contracts your muscles, stifles your voice, and creates disturbing thoughts. When you realize how you let fear control your life, then you can transform it into more pleasurable emotions.

Relax in spite of fear. Allow your body to move when you are afraid. Movement turns fear into energy. Let the tingling turn into joy as you approach the feared object with open arms. The feared object may be a person, an animal, a part of your environment, or anything that creates fear in you. This technique works even when the feared object is not physically present. Visualize yourself approaching the feared object as if you were going to embrace it, and infuse it with all of the love you can summon. You will no doubt discover that much of your fear is imaginary.

Even in truly dangerous situations, fear does not help your performance but impedes it. Fear may act as a warning signal to assist you in avoiding some danger. But, even then you could use your intuition and avoid the wear and tear on your body.

So realize that fear is synonymous with blocking

the energy flow in your body or withdrawing your ki. When approaching your fear with love, you are simultaneously extending ki. Let your power radiate, and your fear will dissolve.

DEVOTION

Devotion to carrying out the laws of the universe means that you will be functioning perfectly in every situation. Only when you completely feel the guidance that the universe provides and experience a profound thankfulness in your heart will you begin to make true progress in aikido.

Each situation you find yourself in is different from any situation that you have experienced or will experience. You need to let go of any rules that your conscious mind has formulated for functioning in similar situations. Each situation is unique. There are no similar circumstances. Your mind only creates similarities so you can feel a false sense of security which lulls you into a life of sameness and robotic patterns. This attitude leads to defeat.

Even the violent person who defeats an opponent in a fight cannot be sure that he will do so in his next encounter. Yet he would feel a false sense of security because he has defeated the man before.

Since you cannot truly feel secure by relying on past experience, how can you feel secure? Trust that all is well and that the universe will take care of you in every situation.

Even the veteran combat soldier can be killed, the star athlete can lose, and the dancer can slip. So let go of confidence and become calm. Let your mental structures of reality dissolve and experience peace. Feel the sun on your face, the wind in your hair, and devotion in your heart.

HUMOR

In order to laugh sincerely, you have to let go. Therefore, laughter is great aikido practice. Practice aikido by listening to Steve Martin records or watching your favorite comedy show. Get together with your friends and allow yourself to experience your natural humor.

Do not take yourself too seriously. Too many people involved in spirituality do. Being able to see humor in even dangerous situations allows you to relax and act harmoniously. It is difficult to remain tense while laughing.

Humor extinguishes anger. If someone is mad at you, make him laugh. Not only would you prevent unnecessary strife, but you may make a friend. All arguments are unnecessary, and humor is an effective tool in dissolving them. A laugh a day keeps the attacker away.

*"...letting go
of your preconceptions
is essential."*

Mind

ATTITUDE

Attitude is the most important ingredient in obtaining self-knowledge. Most of the beliefs you now hold are blatant illusions that can be dismissed with the wave of a hand. However, you cling to them with the ferocity of a tiger.

A nonclinging and receptive attitude is a prerequisite for the successful study of aikido. Have you ever observed your mind long enough to notice all the fighting that goes on between the various parts of yourself? If you are honest with yourself, you will notice that you have conflicting opinions within yourself on most important issues. The reason for this is that you have no idea of who you are.

If you have had an emotional reaction or have been offended by what has been written so far, it shows that you need work on your attitude. The universe is not concerned with the triviality of your thoughts. It demands total dedication to the development of your inner potential.

Have you ever totally committed yourself to anything? Probably not. Your mind may have convinced you that you have, but you probably have not.

49

Commitment to letting go of your preconceptions is essential. The universe is not predictable in its teaching. You need to be open to the moment-to-moment teaching it offers. Every activity that you engage in can be a teaching.

Stop seeing what you want to see and start to see what is really there. The result will surely startle and amaze you. The truth will surely shock you. If you are willing to unlearn what you have learned, then you will have an easy time studying aikido.

NONATTACHMENT

Everything in this world changes. To resist change is useless and time-consuming. In order to live effortlessly and happily, you need to flow with your changes. The only other choice is suffering.

If you were to thoroughly examine all that you value, you would find that most of it is just a heavy load. After discarding your unnecessary baggage, what remains is your individual purpose on this planet. This and your relationships with the people who are here to assist you in fulfilling your destiny are important. Most other things are just trivial concerns.

Your attachments affect everything you do, including self-defense. If you are attached to approval from others, you may have difficulty being spontaneous. If you lack spontaneity while being attacked, you may not find the perfect movement to reconcile the attack.

One illustrative incident stands out in my mind. I talked a friend into coming to our karate class. He was excessively afraid of getting hurt. Well, sure enough, he broke a bone in his hand during his first lesson. His attachment was not only to avoiding injury but to proving himself right. He caused an "accident" in order to show himself and others that he had good reason not to engage in karate and physical sports in general. He did not participate in other sports. He was ruled by his belief.

You are controlled by your attachments. You have surely heard of people who have been killed protecting a piece of property or an idea. If you examine your ideas, you will find that they determine who your friends are, where you live, and almost everything else you do. Yet many of your ideas have been handed down to you from other people such as parents, friends, and authority figures. You have never examined or questioned many of them. They control you. Only when you let go of what you think you know and tune into a power greater than yourself will you be truly nonattached.

QUALITY

The quality of your thoughts is more important than the quantity. After all, if you clutter your mind with too many useless thoughts, you would need a garbage truck to carry your head around. Quantity of thoughts contributes to a sensation of heaviness, quality of thoughts to a sensation of lightness.

If you want to stop feeling tired, examine the quality of your thoughts. Start with the category of noninterference. Noninterference means not imposing your beliefs on others. Without thoughts of interference, you will have a lot of free time on your hands. You do not think so? Remember, even thinking that people should believe as you do falls into the category of interference.

When observing the conflicting thoughts that arise in your mind, choose the one that leads to a feeling of lightness and noninterference. Note that a "positive" thought, if not true, is not the same as a quality thought. A quality thought will have the feeling of peace and letting go associated with it. Whereas a positive thought, if misleading, will give you a false sense of excitement that leaves you open to a fall into depression when the illusion shatters.

You may only want to share your quality thoughts with people who understand them and have some of their own. Otherwise, you may find that your thoughts make the other person examine his own mind, even momentarily. He may not like what he finds and resent you for it. Remember the principle of noninterference when sharing quality thoughts.

How does this pertain to aikido? A noninterfering mind will not draw attention to itself. If you are not telepathically interfering with another person's mental space, then you have less chance of securing his wrath. Noninterference leads to not being attacked.

How about mental or verbal attacks? If a person is thinking negatively about you or verbally abusing you, you may want to try silence. If you quiet your mind and do not speak, then the attacker's thoughts and words will rebound back to him. After all, his agitation only reflects his own temporary inharmony. His thoughts or statements do not accurately describe your essence. Let the universe teach him the inaccuracy of his behavior through your silence.

An attack is only an attack if you perceive it as an attack. Rather than perceiving negative thoughts and words as attacking, perceive them as momentary reflections of the pain that the attacking individual is feeling. This way of perceiving opens up your empathy so that it is easier for you not to be offended. No offense, no attack.

This principle applies to physical attacks as well. Unless you have physically or mentally injured your attacker, he probably is not attacking you anyway. He may be symbolically attacking his father, mother, or someone else that may have caused him pain. Do not take it personally. If you do not unconsciously take on the specific role in the attacker's mind and play the part that he wants you to play, then his attack will not obtain the desired result. He will break off the attack or lose interest. Remember, it is important to avoid attack in the first place by having the quality of your thoughts radiating noninterference, peace, and harmony.

"Spirit...
knows no limitations..."

Spirit

INTUITION

If you follow your intuition your life will be an effortless adventure. You can dance gracefully from moment to moment without frustration and suffering.

The first step in allowing your intuition to direct your life is knowing when to use your logical mind. Logic is fine for balancing your checkbook, using a street map, and other mundane tasks. However, when it comes to enjoying each moment, your intuition is the answer.

One of the failings in using the logical mind for decision-making is that you never have enough data to make a clear decision. Intuition has access to more information than you can imagine. So it is logical for you to use your intuition.

Whenever your conscious mind is relaxing, you are able to be intuitive. As soon as you consciously attempt to control what you are intuitively receiving, the connection will be broken. In fact, whenever you consciously try to rule your life in any way, your intuition will remain silent.

Intuition is a direct channel from your spirit. Spirit is the part of you that knows no limitations and is connected to a power greater than itself. Why live like a snail in a box when there are inner galaxies to be explored? Give your spirit wings by following its intuitive guidance. The only limitations lie in your mind.

POWER

The amount of power available to you in each situation is dependent upon what you are planning to use it for. If you gain power only to use it for show and the enhancement of your own personal ego, then you will eventually lose it. On the other hand, if you become solely guided by the universe, then you will be given the power to successfully carry out its will. This means that many of your actions will benefit others and not yourself. You may find yourself in unexpected situations performing in unpredictable ways, and yet everything turns out perfectly.

In order to correctly channel the power of the universe, you need to go into each situation without expectations. If you could perform an aikido throw perfectly yesterday, do not expect to do so today. Yet paradoxically, the attitude of having no expectations leads to the perfect execution of the throw. Rather than interfering with the power of the universe through conscious expectation, you become an empty channel allowing perfect actions to become manifest.

It is important to remember that it is the power

of the universe that nourishes your spirit and keeps you alive. Without that energy, your breath would cease. It is a gift to live even for another moment. Show your respect for your gift of life by only using your power for the benefit of mankind and not for personal gain.

PRESENCE

The way in which you live contributes to your personal presence. Presence is the aura of energy surrounding your body as well as the reflection of your spiritual essence. Your essence is with you before birth, and how you shape it is based upon your conscious or unconscious choices during this lifetime. If you speak and act truthfully, you will shape your essence in one manner. If you live by illusions and lies, your essence will become distorted. Your presence will reflect the quality of your essence.

Presence is not facade. Certain politicians and other individuals who speak to deceive will utilize their power to weave a facade that impresses the common man. It will feed the common man's limited conceptions of what is good and right. In this way, some men gain power over people. A facade can be shattered by truth, presence cannot. Quality presence is built on a foundation of truth.

When practicing aikido, you infuse your essence with the qualities of peace, love, and harmony. After a period of time, these qualities take hold and reflect themselves in how strong your biofield of energy (ki) is. An essence containing truly positive qualities will be reflected in a presence that affects everything in its midst. This is why a teacher can teach without words. Something is transmitted by his personal presence.

Do not have undue concern if you feel afraid around such an individual. It is only because you are like a one amp capacity wire receiving a 100 amp current. You are receiving a tremendous input of energy. Relax and enjoy the input. It is an important step in the development of your own presence.

As you continue the development of your presence, your life becomes less work and more fun. Your energy seems to have increased tenfold. People wonder how you can accomplish so much. What is most important is that you have become a vehicle for stimulating positive change in people by merely being among them. Now you are able to relax and let your presence do the teaching.

"...we are all beginners."

Martial Arts

STUDY

Many people begin to study the martial arts because of fear. They are afraid of being injured by an aggressor or forced into unpleasant situations. They think they are incapable of defending themselves adequately without proper study of techniques. That is just not so.

I have students of self-mastery who obtain knowledge of themselves before formally studying aikido. When they begin their study, they find that they already know it. Their ki is impressively strong, and they have an intuitive feel for sensing an attack before it begins.

So rather than beginning with the physical techniques of the martial arts and possibly becoming a scared and efficient fighting machine, choose to develop your knowledge of self. You can study techniques anytime.

BELTS

The universe does not give material credentials to the teachers of its way, and neither do I give belts to my students. There are important reasons for this.

If a beginning student comes into class and sees upper belts performing a technique flawlessly he unconsciously deduces, "Yes, they can do that perfectly because of their rank, but I am just a beginner so I cannot." The beginner unconsciously feels that he should not offend the upper belts by performing as well as them. Without belts, I have seen beginners perform certain techniques better than advanced students.

If aikido is truly to be studied to gain self-knowledge, then belts are not only unnecessary but a hindrance. If a person's ego gets caught up in his rank, he will find it difficult to progress. The people who can see his knowledge will learn from him whether he has a belt or not.

In studying the lessons of the universe in general and aikido in particular, we are all beginners. As the mystery unfolds, we learn more and simultaneously experience that we know less. The lessons are infinite and varied.

Why should we beginners wear belts unless they are for holding up our pants. Let us study together in an atmosphere of noncompetition, unity, and friendship.

KI

Ki is the energy that flows harmoniously through your body when your mind is calm and concentrated. The ki of the universe and your ki are one and the same. Consciously experiencing and developing your ki can lead to effortless self-defense.

In Phoenix, I wrote a magazine article about one of my students who epitomizes the correct utilization of ki. I would like to share an excerpt from that article with you.

It is hard to believe that a small twelve-year-old boy cannot be lifted by two grown men, and the same men can be spontaneously thrown across the room after attacking him. This boy, Paul, is in harmony with the universe, and every attack must dissipate its force against such awesome power. More important, however, is that Paul loves his attackers. Everyone is his friend. At school when a hostile boy attempts to push him, he pushes empty air. Before his surprised look subsides, Paul tells him that he does not want to fight, but to be his friend. The boy rides off confused and perhaps wiser after witnessing the power of love.

Paul is a member of Polestar's ki development class, where he learns that a calm mind,
loving heart, and strong spirit are more powerful than brute force. Using numerous energy-
flow exercises that physically test and develop
the strength of his ki, he progresses further in
grace, power, and strength each week. Paul
learns aikido throws and holds to aid him in
the understanding and usefulness of his new-
found strength. More important, however, is
that Paul learns a philosophy of love that will
sustain him not only in defense of his body,
but in his spiritual journey through life.

*"How to be a conscious
individual in robot world..."*

Games

BEING CENTERED

Centered means being bodily relaxed, emotionally calm, mentally concentrated, spiritually aware, and much more. Most people do not understand the concept and spend a lot of time and energy pretending to be centered. They think, "A spiritual person is centered. Therefore, if I want to be spiritual, I have to act centered." They receive approval and silent applause from the other members of their specific group who are playing the same game.

Being centered requires knowing who you are. A person who is himself is totally unpredictable. He can be emotionally calm while angry or aware while appearing not aware.

So when practicing aikido, it is not enough to be just relaxed, calm, and aware. You need to listen to your inner rhythm that spontaneously directs your responses.

For example, when I was 17 years old and just released from boot camp, I arrived at my new duty station. As was the custom of the barracks toughs, I was tested to see what sturdy stuff I was made of. While they were having fun verbally trying to anger me, I was amused. They were quite humorous and entertaining. Their leader began to make some negative statements about my mother when I got a serious look on my face. I solemnly said, "My mother's dead." There was a deep silence until one of them noticed that I had a slight grin on my face. He pointed that out to the others, and they simultaneously began laughing at the leader who was looking a little sheepish. When the laughter subsided, they dispersed and never troubled me again. Actually, they were thereafter quite friendly. All because I had allowed the perfect response to emerge spontaneously from my mouth. Of course, my mother was not dead but very much alive. Had I tried to pretend to be centered instead of being myself, the situation could have turned out quite differently.

Do not attempt to judge the wisdom of the universe when it moves through you. Just be natural and let your actions be spontaneous. Centeredness will follow.

ROBOTS

The robot game is an amazing and intriguing game to observe. It is played by people of all ages, and its stakes are high. You lose your mind and spirit.

If you desire, you can begin from birth. Just pick a person who is rigid of body, emotionally dead, and continually talking about the same subjects. Then imitate him. Sound easy? Look around at all the players. If you do not start playing early, you can easily catch up when you reach school age. In fact, your teachers and friends will encourage you.

What if you just do not want to play? Sorry, not many alternatives available. Except one. To be yourself. Sure, you can still play with your mechanical friends. You may influence them to stop their game if only for a moment. After all, they may have forgotten that it is a game and thank you.

Do not count on it. You will most likely receive standard communication tape 15 explaining how you have changed and are different now. You were much nicer before. If your friend is a serious player, you may receive standard communication tape 15 A on how you should be locked up for your own protection.

You may ask, "How to be a conscious individual in robot world, that is the question." Or more specifically, "Do I have to practice aikido with robots?" Actually that would be too easy. Practicing aikido with the proper teacher and in the right atmosphere appears to help people discover themselves. You do have to sweep up the discarded mechanical parts after class, but that is included in the price of the class. You can sell the workable parts to TV repair shops.

If you can laugh at this, then you will enjoy studying aikido or watching the original Saturday Night Live series. Check our special class rates for wild and crazy guys. Wild and crazy women and children will also receive discounts. Robot rates are currently unavailable.

GO

Go is a Japanese game that consists of black and white stones and a board of 361 points (19 by 19 intersecting lines). The object is to obtain as much space (territory) as possible. You can also take your opponent's stones off the board by surrounding them.

In order to let the game teach you aikido, you must have a nonattached attitude. The player who attacks can easily lose his perspective of the whole board and may win a minor battle but will lose the game. Your stones need to be placed so that they work harmoniously together to accomplish a larger purpose. A stone placed anywhere on the board has its influence (ki) radiating in all directions and can affect distant parts of the board. Your opening moves cannot be planned and calculated as exactly as in chess. They must be intuitive to be effective. Go is training for the intuition and a great way to learn nonresistance, spontaneity, and effortlessness.

"You begin to know things
that you have not learned..."

The Way

NONVIOLENCE

It is natural to be nonviolent. Have you ever noticed that butterflies appear in your stomach and your body becomes tense just thinking about physical conflict? Even verbal conflict is most unpleasant. Your body seems to be repelled by conflict.

However, your mind may think differently. You may have been taught that competition is healthy, man is naturally aggressive, and other such garbage. If you have not thoroughly examined such ideas, you may still believe them.

False ideas cause a conflict between the mind and body. A relaxed body is intuitive. If you learn to trust the intuitive messages that your body sends you, then you will not harm yourself or others.

Harming yourself may take many forms. You may drink too much, smoke, overeat, or place unnecessary stresses on your body. Or, you may harm yourself more subtly. You might use thoughts to criticize yourself and make yourself feel bad. Any form of self-harm is unnecessary.

If you eliminate self-deprecating thoughts from

your mind, you will begin to like and even love yourself. Once this change occurs, then its natural extension is to become more compassionate toward all forms of life. Many people become vegetarians at this point. Once you give up your past conditioning and open yourself up to your deep feelings, you will discover that all life is sacred. Open your heart to your own natural gentleness.

FRIENDSHIP

The circle of people that you consider as your friends changes as your consciousness evolves. Initially, you may feel sad when this happens, but intuitively you know that it is part of your growth. Attempting to hold on to old ties that are no longer meaningful is futile in the long run. It only leads to frustration and suffering.

Once your vision expands past the barriers and blockades of traditional thought, you will be on your own in relatively unexplored territory. You may desire companions to travel with you on your journey into consciousness. As you begin your search, you may run into spiritual groups offering friendship and acceptance only if you conform to their way of thinking. When you decide that you would rather travel alone than with false friends, the universe opens a whole new world of possibilities for you.

Unexpectedly, you begin meeting people who share your uncompromising quest for truth. As more and more people fill your life, you realize that one circle of friends has fallen away to be replaced by a new circle. Such is the way of the universe.

Studying aikido can help make your transition easier. Many people do not come to study aikido solely to learn self-defense techniques, but to meet people of like mind. Sometimes your new circle of friends can be found through the people that you meet while studying aikido, sometimes not. But, whether or not you find a new circle of friends by attending classes, you will be making a mental preparation for meeting them in the future by studying the aikido principles of nonresistance to change and acceptance of the universal will.

SELF-MASTERY

When you reach a certain level of awareness, you realize that there is more to life than success, power, and the rewards that money can bring. You want to know the reason for your existence, the purpose for your life. External concerns dwindle in importance as your inner life takes on a new meaning. You begin to feel directed by a power greater than yourself.

How soon you reach this stage of development depends on your level of evolution, but the journey onward is the same. You need to examine your conceptions of reality with a fine-tooth comb and discard the conceptions that no longer serve your inner direction. You become like a wonder-filled child, knowing that all of the knowledge you have gathered until now has become worthless compared to the vastness that awaits you. Discovering and exploring your inner reality becomes a driving force in your life. At this point, there is a need to have a knowledgeable teacher and a proven method to aid you in the development of your consciousness. Self-Mastery is such a method.

Self-Mastery consists of a series of sessions or interactions between student and teacher. During these sessions, the evolution of your consciousness is rapidly accelerated. Your illusions are shattered and you become more natural and spontaneous, relying on your intuition for guidance. You begin to know things that you have not learned and begin to have experiences beyond your present conceptions. Your life becomes an adventure and journey into the unknown.

What do self-mastery and aikido have in common? They are identical in conception and different in practice. Just as any method becomes a reflection of those who teach it, so it is with aikido.

My students learn that nonviolence is more powerful than violence and that aikido is a way of life. Some students begin studying aikido as their first step in self-development. They begin with the outer movements and continue with the study of inner aikido, self-mastery. Other students begin with self-mastery and study aikido to master their body and energy body.

Of course, self-defense is present in the study of aikido. It just is not paramount in importance. Our classes are enjoyable. They are filled with ease and humor. Everyone feels at home. The self-defense techniques are effortlessly absorbed in an atmosphere of friendship and cooperation.

So students of self-mastery and aikido study together harmoniously. There is an unspoken knowledge conveyed to the beginner as he waits to begin his first lesson: "You are here to discover what you already know — how to defend yourself without even trying."

ABOUT THE AUTHOR

Terry Chitwood was born on November 10, 1947, in Milwaukee, Wisconsin. He graduated from high school at 17 and joined the service. During his tour of duty, he was in Guam, the Philippine Islands, Japan, and Vietnam. He graduated in 1972 from the University of Wisconsin (Milwaukee) magna cum laude with a B.A. in psychology. He received his M.A. in counseling psychology from the University of South Dakota in 1974. He graduated from the University of South Dakota in 1976 with an Ed.D. degree in counseling psychology.

Dr. Chitwood worked as a psychologist at Plains Area Mental Health Center, LeMars, Iowa; Redfield State Hospital, Redfield, South Dakota; West Iowa Mental Health Center, Carroll, Iowa; and the Ft. Grant Training Center (minimum security prison), Ft. Grant, Arizona. He developed the Polestar prison program at Ft. Grant where hardcore convicts were transformed into loving individuals. The program consisted of the following modalities: yoga, aikido, tai chi, rebirthing, postural restructuring, self-mastery, and a variety of psychological therapies. Dr. Chitwood is the founder of postural restructuring, a connective tissue and muscle manipulation system that releases bodily tension, relieves mental stress and straightens the posture. He is also the founder of self-mastery, an effective method for spiritual development.

After making the prison program self-perpetuating, Dr. Chitwood started his own business in Phoenix called Polestar. He used the same modalities as in the prison program to help intelligent and self-aware individuals evolve their consciousness. Presently, he is working with his students through Polestar in Sioux Falls, South Dakota, where he specializes in postural restructuring, self-mastery and aikido.

ABOUT POLESTAR

If you enjoyed this book and desire more information about our other publications, tapes, sessions, and seminars, please contact us at the following address:

Polestar
620 South Minnesota
Sioux Falls, SD 57104